Tarsier

by Dawn Bluemel Oldfield

Consultant: Thane Maynard, Director
Cincinnati Zoo and Botanical Garden
Cincinnati, Ohio

BEARPORT
PUBLISHING

New York, New York

Credits

Cover, © outcast85/Shutterstock; TOC, © Holger Mette/iStock; 4–5, © Bambara/Shutterstock; 6–7, © szefei/Shutterstock; 6T, © AndamanSE/iStock; 7L, © outcast85/Shutterstock; 7R, © Natursports/Shutterstock; 8T, © Art Phaneuf Photography/Shutterstock; 8B, © vlad09/Shutterstock; 9, © michael williams/Alamy Stock Photo; 10–11, © Nature Picture Library/Alamy Stock Photo; 12, © Ondrej Prosicky/Shutterstock; 13, © imageBROKER/Alamy Stock Photo; 14, © Andrey Zvoznikov/ardea.com; 15, © dpa picture alliance/Alamy Stock Photo; 16L, © BOONCHUAY PROMJIAM/Shutterstock; 16R, © lendy16/Shutterstock; 17, © Frans Lanting/Danita Delimont/ardea.com; 18, © Andrey Zvoznikov/ardea.com; 19, © Andrey Zvoznikov/ardea.com; 20, © Rhett A. Butler/mongabay.com; 21, © Masahiro Iijima/ardea.com; 22T, © Cynthia Kidwell/Shutterstock; 22M, © jaana piira/Shutterstock; 22B, © ammmit/Depositphotos; 23TL, © alexsvirid/Shutterstock; 23TR, © Andrea Izzotti/Shutterstock; 23BL, © Jurgen Vogt/Shutterstock; 23BR, © Signature Message/Shutterstock.

Publisher: Kenn Goin
Editor: Jessica Rudolph
Creative Director: Spencer Brinker
Design: Debrah Kaiser
Photo Researcher: Olympia Shannon

Library of Congress Cataloging-in-Publication Data

Names: Bluemel Oldfield, Dawn, author.
Title: Tarsier / by Dawn Bluemel Oldfield.
Description: New York, New York : Bearport Publishing, [2016] | Series: Weird but cute | Audience: Ages 4–8._ | Includes bibliographical references and index.
Identifiers: LCCN 2015040014| ISBN 9781943553280 (library binding) | ISBN 1943553289 (library binding)
Subjects: LCSH: Tarsiers—Juvenile literature.
Classification: LCC QL737.P965 B58 2016 | DDC 599.8/3—dc23
LC record available at http://lccn.loc.gov/2015040014

For more information, write to Bearport Publishing Company, Inc., 45 West 21st Street, Suite 3B, New York, New York 10010. Printed in the United States of America.

10 9 8 7 6 5 4 3 2 1

Contents

What's this weird
but cute animal?

It's a
tarsier.

BIG eyes!

Long fingers and toes! **5**

Tarsiers (TAHR-see-uhrz) are found in Asia.

They live in warm **rain forests**.

There are many different kinds of tarsiers.

spectral tarsier

rain forest

western tarsier

Philippine tarsier

7

Tarsiers are very small.

They weigh about as much as an apple!

Did you know tarsiers are **nocturnal**?

Their big eyes help them see in the dark.

Tarsiers have great eyesight and hearing.

Unlike people, tarsiers can't move their eyes.

They move their heads instead.

A tarsier's eyeball is as big as its brain!

Tarsiers can turn their heads all the way around to look behind them!

Hop, hop!

Tarsiers are good jumpers.

They leap from tree to tree.

Tarsiers can leap more than 16 feet (5 m)! Their long fingers and toes help them grab tree branches.

Munch, munch, munch!

Tarsiers eat **insects** such as crickets.

They also eat small birds and bats.

bat

bird

How does a tarsier catch its food?

It grabs a critter with its hands.

Tarsiers can grab flying birds or insects right out of the air!

Then the tarsier kills the animal with its sharp teeth.

butterfly

Baby tarsiers are very tiny.

Yet at one day old, they can already climb trees.

Soon they'll be able to leap just like their parents!

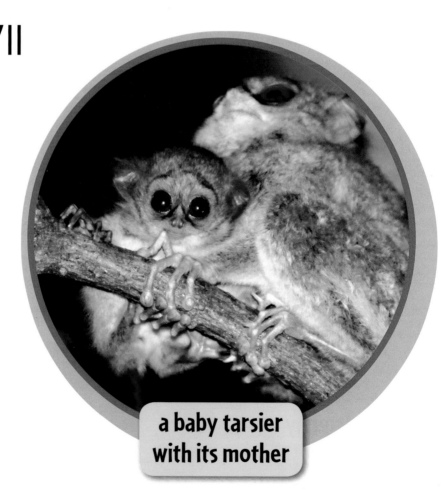

a baby tarsier with its mother

More Weird Primates

Emperor Tamarin

The emperor tamarin lives in rain forests in South America. Because of its very long, white mustache, this monkey is thought to look like some human emperors!

Howler Monkey

The howler monkey lives in rain forests in Central America and South America. It is the loudest monkey in the world. Its howl can be heard up to 4 miles (6.5 km) away!

Owl Monkey

The owl monkey lives in rain forests in Central America and South America. It looks like an owl that always seems to be smiling.

Glossary

insects (IN-sekts) small animals that have six legs, two antennae, three main body parts, and a hard covering

nocturnal (nok-TUR-nuhl) active mainly at night

primates (PRYE-mayts) members of a group of animals that includes humans, monkeys, apes, and lemurs

rain forests (RAYN FOR-ists) warm areas of land covered with trees and other plants, where lots of rain falls

Index

Read More

Leaf, Christina. *Tarsier (Extremely Weird Animals).* Minneapolis, MN: Bellwether Media (2014).

Van Eck, Thomas. *Tarsiers in the Dark (Creatures of the Night).* New York: Gareth Stevens (2013).

Learn More Online

To learn more about tarsiers, visit
www.bearportpublishing.com/WeirdButCute

About the Author

Dawn Bluemel Oldfield is a writer. She enjoys reading, traveling, and gardening. She and her husband live in Prosper, Texas, where unfortunately there are no tarsiers.